W9-BVV-470

POP CULTURE BIOS
★ SUPERSTARS

VICTORIA
JUSTICE

TELEVISION'S IT GIRL

JODY JENSEN SHAFFER

⌐ Lerner Publications Company
MINNEAPOLIS

For Alison, Annette, Carolyn,
Judith, Mona, Rachel, and Sheri

Lerner Publications Company
A division of Lerner Publishing Group, Inc.
241 First Avenue North
Minneapolis, MN 55401 U.S.A.

Website address: www.lernerbooks.com

Library of Congress Cataloging-in-Publication Data

Shaffer, Jody Jensen.
        Victoria Justice : television's it girl / by Jody Jensen Shaffer.
            p.   cm. — (Pop culture bios: superstars)
        Includes index.
        ISBN 978–1–4677–1309–2 (lib. bdg. : alk. paper)
        ISBN 978–1–4677–1772–4 (eBook)
        1. Justice, Victoria, 1993– Juvenile literature. 2. Actors—United States—Juvenile literature. 3. Singers—United States—Juvenile literature. I. Title.
    PN2287.J87S53 2014
    791.4502'8092—dc23 [B]   2013001167

Manufactured in the United States of America
1 – BP – 7/15/13

INTRODUCTION

Colored stage lights flash and blink. The band starts to play. Screams of anticipation echo across the sold-out amphitheater. Suddenly Victoria Justice appears behind a large piece of canvas. Her fans erupt. As the screen drops, Victoria belts out "Make It Shine." It's the theme song from her hit TV show, *Victorious*.

As she dances across the stage, the star touches the hands of those lucky enough to be in the first row. One excited fan almost pulls Victoria into the pit! Victoria laughs. **"Not quite yet,"** she says. **"We have a few more songs to do!"** The star spins around, grabs the mic, and gives her fans what they came for.

Victoria poses with her mom, Serene, at an event in 2011.

CHAPTER ONE

NATURAL PERFORMER

Victoria and her sister, Madison, rock the red carpet in 2005.

Victoria Dawn Justice was born in Hollywood, Florida, on February 19, 1993. Her parents are Serene and Zack Justice. Victoria's younger sister, Madison, came along three years later. When Victoria and her sister were little, their parents divorced. Their mom later married the girls' stepdad, Mark Reed.

Victoria was always performing for her family. She loved to sing and put on one-person shows. When Victoria was eight, she saw a boy about her age in a potato chip ad. She told her mom she wanted to be on TV too. Serene knew how much her daughter loved performing, so she took Victoria seriously. She got Victoria an agent. The agent got auditions for Victoria. Victoria's first audition was for an ad for Ovaltine, the chocolate milk powder. She took a container of the powder to her audition and landed the job!

AGENT =
a person who finds jobs for people who want to act

AUDITION =
a short performance by an actor trying out for a role

Victoria adored being in front of the camera. She decided she wanted to give modeling a try. She tried out for and got modeling gigs with several big-name companies. Guess, Ralph Lauren, Unionbay, and Gap were among them.

Since fashion labels seemed eager to hire her, Victoria began to wonder if even bigger jobs might be a possibility. She wondered if she could land a part in a TV show or a movie. Victoria's mom thought she could. She had a gut feeling that her daughter could really flourish as an actor. Serene wanted to give her daughter every chance to succeed. So in 2003, she and her husband took a drastic step. They picked up and moved their family to Hollywood, California, where most major auditions are held.

Victoria and her family moved from beautiful Hollywood, Florida (LEFT), to Hollywood, California, to follow Victoria's dreams.

From Hollywood to Hollywood

After just three weeks in California, Victoria scored a guest appearance on the TV show *Gilmore Girls*. Other jobs didn't follow right away, but Victoria made a splash in other ways. She was accepted into a musical theater school called Millikan. All the students there loved to sing, act, and dance. Victoria fit right in.

After Victoria started attending Millikan, more jobs began to open up. She played a character named Stella in a short film called *Mary.* She had a cameo in the TV movie *When Do We Eat?* She played Rose in Hallmark's *Silver Bells* on CBS. And soon, Victoria landed her favorite gig yet. She got to guest star on *The Suite Life of Zack and Cody*, an extremely popular show on the Disney Channel.

CAMEO =
a brief appearance

KISS & TELL

Victoria's first-ever on-screen kiss was with Cole Sprouse on *The Suite Life of Zack and Cody.*

Victoria poses with *Suite Life* stars Dylan (LEFT) and Cole Sprouse in 2010.

Zoey 101

Victoria's big break came in 2005. She auditioned for Nickelodeon producer Dan Schneider. He cast her as Lola Martinez in *Zoey 101*, starring Jamie Lynn Spears. The show was about girls joining an all-boys boarding school. Victoria was thrilled!

Victoria loved every second of working on *Zoey 101*. She adored her character. She also learned a lot on the set, such as how cameras work, how to read lines, and how to be professional.

Victoria snagged even more acting jobs in 2006. She won a guest role on TV's *Everwood*. She had a cameo in the movie *Unknown*. She played Holly in the movie *The Garden*.

But Victoria did more than act. When she was fourteen, she decided to try her hand at a singing career.

FROM LEFT: (TOP ROW) Sean Flynn, Matthew Underwood, and Chistopher Massey; (CENTER ROW) Erin Sanders, Jamie Lynn Spears, and Victoria; and (BOTTOM) Paul Butcher—the cast of *Zoey 101*

Victoria (LEFT) and Jamie Lynn Spears appear on a 2006 episode of Zoey 101.

She'd loved to sing ever since she was little and would perform for her family. Like everything else Victoria had tried, her singing career was a success! In 2007, she recorded and released her first song, a cover of Vanessa Carlton's "A Thousand Miles."

HELLO, BOOKWORM?

When she was in middle school, Victoria didn't go to parties. And she didn't care about looking good all the time. Instead, she and her best friend would call each other and read chapters of *Twilight* together over the phone.

COVER =
a new performance of a popular song

Victoria and costar
Simon Curtis sign
autographs for fans
of *Spectacular!*
in 2009.

CHAPTER TWO

ENDINGS AND BEGINNINGS

Victoria performs in a flash mob promoting *Victorious* in 2011.

On May 2, 2008, Victoria experienced a big change in her life. Zoey 101 was canceled. Victoria's run as Lola Martinez ended. "I was so sad, I didn't know how I was going to get over it," Victoria said. But bigger things were yet to come for her.

Nickelodeon asked producer Dan Schneider to develop another project for Victoria. She and her mom met Schneider for dinner. Victoria told Schneider she attended a performing arts school. Schneider liked the idea. He began creating a show around it. **"I'm the type of kid who was never afraid to look really silly on camera,"** Victoria spilled. "[Dan] enjoyed that. He also found out that I like to sing, and he drew inspiration from that."

Dan Schneider is a producer, writer, and actor who started his career in the mid-1980s.

Spectacular!

In 2009 Victoria auditioned for a role in the Nickelodeon movie *Spectacular!* Even though she knew the movie's producers from her previous Nickelodeon work, they didn't just hand Victoria a part. **"I had to audition like everybody else,"** she explained. "I had to go through three callbacks, and it was not easy. In the end, I'm so glad I did it, and it was so much fun."

Victoria got the role of Tammi in the film. *Spectacular!* aired on February 16, 2009. More than 3.7 million people saw it. Victoria also scored appearances in Nickelodeon's *The Naked Brothers Band, iCarly, BrainSurge,* and *The Troop.*

Four members of the *Spectacular!* cast—Tammin Sursok, Simon Curtis, Victoria, and Nolan Funk—head out to the MTV Video Music Awards.

With her busy work schedule, Victoria found it hard to keep going to regular school. She left Millikan after ninth grade. She was homeschooled until she earned her high school diploma in 2010 at the age of seventeen.

VICTORIA <3S...

- her family
- hanging out with friends
- going to movies
- her dogs, Sophie and Sammy
- sushi, rice and chicken, rice and pork, fried plantains, and KFC
- amusement parks
- feathers
- making her little sister laugh
- turquoise

Victorious

Around the same time Victoria was finishing school, she got some super-exciting news. Dan Schneider had finished creating his show about the performing arts school. He wanted Victoria to be its star. She heard the news after flying to Florida to visit her grandma. Victoria remembers "freaking out" in the airport.

In the show, *Victorious*, Victoria plays high schooler Tori Vega. She attends Hollywood Arts High. Tori discovers her singing and dancing talent after another character gets sick and Tori has to fill in for her onstage.

Victoria sings her heart out on the first episode of *Victorious*.

The first day of production was amazing for Victoria. It happened to be her sixteenth birthday. **"I couldn't believe that I was standing there with all of these people, and it was for my TV show,"** Victoria recalled. "It was everything I had worked so hard for, for all this time, and it made me feel so good. I burst into tears because I was so incredibly happy."

Victoria poses with her surprise birthday cake from the *Victorious* cast and crew in 2012.

Victorious debuted on March 27, 2010. Nearly 6 million people tuned in. The show was Nickelodeon's second-best live action debut of all time.

A LITTLE PRIVACY, PLEASE

Victoria likes to keep her personal life private. No one knows much about whom she's dated. But Victoria has been spotted with a number of good-looking guys, including Josh Hutcherson (RIGHT), Nicholas Hoult, and Ryan Rottman.

Victoria not only starred in *Victorious*, but she also sang its theme song, "Make It Shine." She later recorded the song so that fans could download it or buy it on CD.

Victoria performed yet another song—"Freak the Freak Out"—on the November 22, 2010, *Victorious* episode. She recorded it shortly after. It was her highest debut. It came in at no. 78 on the *Billboard* Hot 100 chart. Victoria also performed the song live at the Macy's Thanksgiving Day Parade.

Victoria rides a float in the 2010 Macy's Thanksgiving Day Parade.

But Victoria didn't leave acting behind. She voiced the character of Stacy the badger on *The Penguins of Madagascar.* She also starred as Jordan Sands, a teenage girl who becomes a werewolf, in the Nickelodeon TV movie *The Boy Who Cried Werewolf.* It drew 5.8 million viewers.

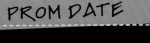

PROM DATE

Although Victoria was on the cover of *Seventeen's* prom issue, she has never been to prom. When a friend held a prom-themed birthday party, Victoria took a guy friend. He gave her a corsage, which made it feel like the real thing!

Victoria (SECOND FROM LEFT) and her castmates from Victorious accept an award in 2012.

CHAPTER THREE

THE SILVER SCREEN

In March 2011, Victoria's acting career kicked into super high gear. She landed the lead in her first feature film, *Fun Size.* Victoria plays teenager Wren. She loses her little brother when they go trick-or-treating on Halloween.

Victoria was pumped that people who had never seen her act before would be able to now. Filming in Cleveland, Ohio, was an amazing experience for Victoria. Since most of the movie takes place on Halloween, the cast filmed at night for two months. The only problem? The movie wouldn't come out for another year! Victoria worked on her music in the meantime.

WHAT AN HONOR!

Victoria got a huge honor on March 31, 2012. *Victorious* won Favorite TV Show at the 2012 Kids' Choice Awards. It was also nominated for Outstanding Children's Program and two other Emmy Awards.

Victoria's character, Wren, finds herself in a sticky situation in this scene from *Fun Size.*

Touring and Making Music

Victoria released the official *Victorious* sound track in August 2012. It debuted at No. 5 on the Top 200 Charts. It came in at No. 2 on the Pop Charts.

Victoria promoted the sound track by going on tour. The Make It In America tour hit seventeen cities. "What I love about the music from the show is it's not little kid music," Victoria noted. "People from age 6 to 45 or 50 can enjoy it. It's a really good show. I'm super proud of it."

When she wasn't performing, Victoria wrote music for her upcoming album. **"I'm just putting my heart and soul into it,"** Victoria said of the project. **"I'm really passionate**

SOUND TRACK = the music from a TV show or a movie

Victoria shows off copies of the *Victorious* sound track.

On September 11, 2012, Victoria bought a house for her family. It was her way of saying thanks for their support. The house has a pool, a Jacuzzi, big closets, and a great backyard.

about it. I love songwriting. It's a creatively fulfilling experience and unlike anything I've done."

Finally, it was premiere day for *Fun Size*. On October 25, 2012, Victoria tweeted, "Today's the big day! The L.A. premiere of @FunSizeMovie. I'm so excited I can barely contain myself! Lol." *Fun Size* premiered at Paramount Studios in L.A. Victoria attended the event with her mom.

DOROTHY X2

As a kid, Victoria went as Dorothy from *The Wizard of Oz* one year for Halloween. "I have a picture of me standing in front of my house with little pigtails and the blue dress my grandma made me," she laughed. What makes that memory extra special for Victoria is that years later, she ended up dressing as Dorothy again (LEFT, WITH COSTAR JANE LEVY) for her part as a trick-or-treater in *Fun Size!*

CHAPTER FOUR

MOVIN' ON

Victoria joins a lineup of famous faces to celebrate Christmas at the White House. FROM LEFT: Conan O'Brien, First Lady Michelle Obama, Sasha Obama, Malia Obama, President Barack Obama, Jennifer Hudson, Victoria, and Justin Bieber.

By late fall 2012, things were changing again for Victoria. After three successful seasons, *Victorious* was canceled. Victoria was shocked. The cast had already filmed fifteen episodes that were scheduled to air in the fourth season. Victoria called her mom to confirm the news.

When Serene told her daughter that *Victorious* really was going off the air, Victoria got really sad. Yet at the same time, she managed to find a bright side to the situation. "Being on *Victorious* was great," she reflected. "But [it was also] super demanding and sometimes grueling because there was music and performances. That added a whole other layer. **I had so much fun, and I loved it, but I think for now I want to continue doing films.**"

BFFL

Victoria's BFFL is her mom. The star says her mom is smart, positive, and fun to be around. Victoria is always asking her mom for advice about her hair, boys, and her career. The two have tons of fun laughing and listening to music together!

On November 28, 2012, Victoria found something else to distract her from the *Victorious* cancelation. She got to kick off the 80th Christmas in Rockefeller Center tree-lighting ceremony in New York City! She sang "Rockin' Around the Christmas Tree" and "Jingle Bells" to millions of fans who showed up in person or tuned in on TV. Victoria later tweeted, **"Omg!! U guys. That was so exciting. Did any of u c my performance just now on NBC?"** Chances are, most of Victoria's Twitter followers had!

Victoria performs for Christmas in Rockefeller Center in 2012.

Doing Good

In addition to her entertainment work, Victoria supports several charities. She believes it's really important to give back. Since 2010, she has worked with the United Nations Foundation's charity, Girl Up. It helps girls in developing countries get education and health care. Victoria also promoted AT&T's It Can Wait campaign. It discourages people from texting and driving. In addition, Victoria joined forces with the Music Makes It Better campaign.

Its goal is to bring music and art to children who are hospitalized.

The Future

Victoria has many big plans for the future. She wants to do more feature films. She'd love to play a variety of characters on-screen. As she explains it, "Being an actress, that's the coolest part—to be able to really explore that world of new characters and show people your range and what you're able to do. I'm looking forward to that."

Victoria also wants to expand her singing career. Her debut solo album is scheduled for release in 2013.

Victoria is excited about the challenges and experiences to come her way. And she's thankful for the opportunities she's had so far. "It's been cool and exciting," she remarked. **"I have amazing memories I can look back on . . . It's something I'm very grateful for."**

WITHOUT WHEELS

Although Victoria is in her twenties, she hasn't had time to learn to drive. She hasn't taken her driving test and doesn't have a license!

VICTORIA PICS!

Victoria (LEFT) hits a red carpet event with her sister, Madison, in 2013.

SOURCE NOTES

5   Autumn McAlpin, "Nickelodeon Star Thrills Young Fans at OC Fair: Victoria Justice Is a Rising Star and Positive Role Model," *Orange County Register*, August 4, 2012.

13   Danielle Scarola, "Victoria's Secrets: Topping Our '10 to Watch' List for 2010, Victoria Justice Is Stepping Out of Her Sidekick Roles and into Superstar Status," *Girls' Life*, December 2009, 46.

13   Amy Robinson, "State Fair All in a Day's Work for Busy Teen Star Victoria Justice," *Charleston (WV) Gazette*, August 16, 2012.

14   Scarola, "Victoria's."

16   Ibid.

17   Ibid.

22   Robinson, "State Fair."

22–23 Ibid.

23   Victoria Justice, Twitter post, October 25, 2012, http://www.twitter.com/VictoriaJustice (February 22, 2013).

23   Madeleine Marr, "Victoria Justice Talks about the Fun of 'Fun Size,'" *Miami Herald*, October 25, 2012.

25   Ibid.

26   Victoria Justice, Twitter post, November 28, 2012, http://www.twitter.com/VictoriaJustice (February 22, 2012).

27   Casey Phillips, "Chattanooga Kidz Expo Guest Victoria Justice Is a Star on the Rise," *Chattanooga Times Free Press*, April 15, 2012.

27   Robinson, "State Fair."

MORE VICTORIA INFO

Leavitt, Amie Jane. *Victoria Justice*. Hockessin, DE: Mitchell Lane, 2011.
This book follows Victoria's life from her childhood through early adulthood.

Nelson, Robin. *Selena Gomez: Pop Star and Actress*. Minneapolis: Lerner Publications, 2013.
Read about another talented young woman who has made a splash both on-screen and in the music world.

Victoria Justice's Official Site
http://victoriajustice.net
On Victoria's site, you can read her latest news, watch videos of interviews, and buy Victoria merchandise.

Victoria on Internet Movie Database
http://www.imdb.com/name/nm1842439/bio
Find out more about Victoria, including her favorite musicals and her nickname.

Victoria on Twitter
https://twitter.com/VictoriaJustice
Follow Victoria as she dishes about what she's wearing, what she's doing, and where she's going.

INDEX

The images in this book are used with the permission of: © Jon Kopaloff/FilmMagic/Getty Images, pp. 2, 27; © Michael Tran/FilmMagic/Getty Images, p. 3 (top), 6 (left); © Jeffrey Mayer/WireImage/Getty Images, pp. 3 (bottom), 29 (bottom left); © Paul Smith/Featureflash/Dreamstime.com, pp. 4 (top left), 29 (top right); © Michael Loccisano/Getty Images, p. 4 (top right); AP Photo/Owen Sweeney/Rex Features, pp. 4 (bottom), 20 (bottom left); © Jason LaVeris/FilmMagic/Getty Images, p. 5; © Theo Wargo/WireImage/Getty Images, p. 6 (right); © Michael Tran/FilmMagic/Getty Images, p. 6; © Imagecollect/Dreamstime.com, p. 7; © Fotomak/Dreamstime.com, p. 8; AP Photo/Vince Bucci, p. 9; © Nickelodeon/Courtesy Everett Collection, p. 10; © Mitchell Haddad/Nickelodeon/Courtesy Everett Collection, p. 11; © Charley Gallay/WireImage/Getty Images, pp. 12 (both), 14; © Michael Buckner/Getty Images for Nickelodeon, p. 13; © Paul Smith/Featureflash/ImageCollect, p. 15; © Lisa Rose/Nickelodeon/Courtesy Everett Collection, p. 16; © Jesse Grant/WireImage/Getty Images, p. 17; © Jeff Kravitz/FilmMagic/Getty Images, p. 18; © Michael Loccisano/Getty Images for Nickelodeon, p. 19; © Michael Buckner/WireImage/Getty Images, p. 20 (top); © Fred Duval/FilmMagic/Getty Images, p. 20 (bottom right); © Jamie Trueblood/Paramount/Courtesy Everett Collection, pp. 21, 23; SUZAN/PA Photos/Landov, p. 22; © Steve Vas/Featureflash/Dreamstime.com, pp. 24 (top left), 28 (top left); © Carrienelson1/Dreamstime.com, p. 24 (top right); AP Photo/Jacquelyn Martin, p. 24 (bottom); Todd Williamson/Invision/AP, p. 25; © Heidi Gutman/NBC/NBCU Photo Bank via Getty Images, p. 26; © Michael Tullberg/Getty Images, p. 28 (bottom left); © Charley Gallay/Getty Images for vitaminwater, p. 28 (right); © KGC-146/starmaxinc.com/ImageCollect, p. 29 (top left); © Chelsea Lauren/WireImage/Getty Images, p. 29 (bottom right).

Front Cover: © Paul Smith/Featureflash/Shutterstock.com; © Gabriel Olsen/FilmMagic/Getty Images.

Back Cover: © Fred Duval/FilmMagic/Getty Images.

Main body text set in Shannon Std Book 12/18.
Typeface provided by Monotype Typography.